DESIGN AND TECHNICAL ART

Richard Spilsbury

Heinemann
LIBRARY

www.heinemann.co.uk/library
Visit our website to find out more information about Heinemann Library books.

To order:
 Phone 44 (0) 1865 888066
Send a fax to 44 (0) 1865 314091
Visit the Heinemann Bookshop at www.heinemann.co.uk/library to browse
our catalogue and order online.

 Produced for Heinemann Library by
White-Thomson Publishing Ltd,
Bridgewater Business Centre,
210 High Street, Lewes,
East Sussex BN7 2NH.

First published in Great Britain by Heinemann Library,
Jordan Hill, Oxford OX2 8EJ, part of Harcourt Education.
Heinemann Library is a registered trademark of
Harcourt Education Ltd.

Editorial: Clare Collinson, Melanie Waldron, Kate Buckingham
Consultant: Susie Hodge
Design: Tim Mayer
Picture Research: Amy Sparks
Production: Chroma Graphics

Originated by Modern Age Ltd
Printed and bound in China by South China Printing Company.

10 digit ISBN: 0 431 01475 2
13 digit ISBN: 978-0-431-01475-3

11 10 09 08 07
10 9 8 7 6 5 4 3 2 1

British Library Cataloguing in Publication Data
Spilsbury, Richard, 1963–
    Design and technical art. – (Art off the wall)
    604.2
A full catalogue record for this book is available from the
British Library.

Acknowledgements
The publisher would like to thank the following for their kind
permission to use their photographs:
Alamy (Michael Booth) p. **50**; Corbis pp. **4** (Noah K. Murray/Star
Ledger), **6** (Jose Luis Pelaez, Inc), **9** (Craig Lovell), **11** (Onne van
der Wal), **16** (Al Fuchs/NewSport), **19** (Robert Levin), **22** (John
Gress/Reuters), **23** (Nayan Sthakiya), **34** (Pitchal Frederic/Corbis
Sygma), **37** (Salvatore Di Nolfi/epa), **38** (Jason Reed/Reuters),
44–45 (Reuters), **48** (Viviane Moos), **51** (Paul Hardy); Getty Images
pp. **17** (AFP), **21** (AFP), **28–29** (MLB Photos), **30**, **33**, **35** (Time Life
Pictures), **41** (AFP), **47**; iStock pp. **7** (Bradley Mason), **27** (Ayaaz
Rattansi); photolibrary p. **25**; Science Photo Library pp. **5** (Philippe
Psaila), **12** (A. Gragera, Latin Stock), **13** (Pasquale Sorrentino),
14 (Rosenfeld Images Ltd), **36** (TRL LTD), **39** (G. Brad Lewis),
42 (James King-Holmes), **43** (NASA); TopFoto/ImageWorks p. **49**.

The artworks on pages 10 and 15 were created by Peter Bull
Art Studio.

Cover photograph reproduced with permission of Science
Photo Library.

Every effort has been made to contact copyright
holders of any material reproduced in this book.
Any omissions will be rectified in subsequent
printings if notice is given to the publishers.

Contents

Words appearing in the text in bold, **like this**, are explained in the Glossary.

Design and technical art

The Kingda Ka roller coaster in New Jersey, United States, is the tallest and fastest on Earth. Designers created it to give people the ride of their lives.

Designers work in every industry on our planet, from leisure and tourism to healthcare. They design things in our homes, from stationery and shelving systems to screws and safety pins. They design multimedia systems and medical instruments. They design vehicles, from cars and skateboards to jet fighters and speedboats. Designers called **architects** create the buildings and bridges around us. Design is a very important part of all our lives.

What is design?

The word design means several different things. The word is sometimes used to refer to how things look. We might say that this pair of trainers or this logo has a better design than another. But design is not just about the way things look on the surface. Even if a car looks great on the outside, it has a bad design if people cannot use it easily or if it does not perform well.

The design process

The word design also refers to the process of translating an idea into something useful. The design process can take a long time. Designers, the people who translate ideas into designs, have to make lots of decisions to get the designs right.

Illustrations are vital to designers because they help visualize what their design ideas will look like when they are made.

Technical art

Technical art is the medium by which designers translate their ideas. **Technical drawings** and **illustrations**, on paper or on computer screen, show in detail what a design is like. They enable others to understand what the design will look like in real life.

Turning ideas into reality

Technical drawings also show people how to make a design into something real. They incorporate detailed, accurate measurements and proportions that can be followed when an object is made. Any idea for a design must have good technical art or it will probably not be turned into reality.

Try it yourself

Throughout this book you will find activities you can try yourself. Most are simple exercises to do with particular stages in the design process. The aim is for you to build up your design skills. You can use the completed exercises as part of a design **portfolio**. This is a collection of your best designs, ideas, and exercises that you keep. It is a record of your development as a designer.

When designers begin the process of turning ideas into reality, they must consider questions as varied as "What is it for?", "Who will use it?", "What will it look like?", and "How can it be made for the right price?" Designers also need to produce detailed technical drawings, illustrations, and models. Manufacturers will use these when they make the designs.

Function and form

The first important question a designer must ask when they have an idea or concept for a design is "What is it for?" The **function** of a product will determine how it is designed. For example, the function of a raincoat is to keep people dry, so the designer must choose waterproof fabric. Designers must also consider the product's **form** – its shape and appearance. People will not buy a raincoat unless they like the way it looks. A product has a good design if its form is well suited to its function.

Designers need to consider both function and form. Generally people will only buy a coat that they like the look of.

Who will use it?

As well as thinking about an object's function and form, a designer must consider who will use the product. Products need to be designed so they are suitable for the people who will use them. For example, a toy for a child who is under three years old must only include parts that are larger than 45 millimetres (1.5 inches). This is to protect the child from the risk of choking on small parts that could be swallowed.

Ergonomics

Designers also need to make their designs safe and easy for people to use. For example, computer workstations need to be designed in a way that enables users to work in comfort. Designers need to consider the position and size of equipment so it is convenient to use. The application of information about the needs of users to the design of furniture, equipment, and environments is called **ergonomics**.

Safety first: egg boxes are designed to keep their contents intact.

Design feature: egg box

Eggs are a fantastic natural food: protein bundled up inside its own shell. The only trouble is that eggshells can easily crack when the eggs are being transported. When this happens, the food inside the egg spoils. In the 1930s, someone came up with an idea for a protective, stackable egg box made out of paper pulp. This material is cheap, light, and recyclable. It can easily be moulded into strong, arched cups to protect the eggs. The same design of egg box is still used today because its form perfectly matches its function – a cheap protective container.

Concept designs

Concept designs are the first basic sketches of a product on paper. Of course, there are lots of ways to draw any concept, so it helps to do a bit of **brainstorming**.

Many designers share their ideas with a group of other people. Each member of the group may suggest different ideas. Some ideas might even seem rather strange, but they may be liked by the group enough to become concept designs.

Consultation

Once one or two concept designs for a new product have been sketched, they are shown to the people who are paying for the product to be designed, the people who will make the product, and those who will sell the product once it has been made.

This consultation is vital because it is a chance for people who are not designers to see the idea. They may suggest ways to alter the design so it will be easier to make or more appealing to buyers.

Getting detailed

The next step in the design process is to prepare precise drawings and illustrations based on the concept designs. The traditional equipment for a designer includes:

- a drafting table that can be angled to make drawing easier

- line guides, including rulers, protractors, and bendable curves – these help designers to draw lines, angles, and shapes accurately

- pens – most designers use sets of pens with tube-shaped nibs to draw accurate ink lines of different widths

- an airbrush and tint sheets – designers add shading and areas of different tones to illustrations using airbrushes, which spray tiny droplets of ink, or tint sheets. Tint sheets are transparent sheets printed with different patterns of dots that are cut out and stuck on to illustrations.

- pencils and paper – designers generally use hard pencils, often 2H grade, to draw accurate lines and they work on smooth paper or tracing paper.

Drawing or illustration?

Designers create both technical drawings and illustrations. So what is the difference? Technical drawings are accurate two-dimensional (2D) depictions of an object showing every detail. They usually show both the front and side views of the object. They are often annotated with labels to explain what the different parts of the object are. Illustrations are different from technical drawings. They depict an object using perspective so the object looks three-dimensional (3D) and is clearly recognizable, without adding every detail.

This designer is using perspective techniques to create a realistic illustration of the front of a ship's deck.

Try it yourself

Your task is to illustrate a building brick to scale, at twice its normal size. For this you will need a toy building brick, such as a Lego brick, a ruler, a pencil, and some paper.

1 Measure and write down the dimensions of the brick. Then double each measurement. Write these measurements down, too.

2 Using the doubled measurements, draw a rectangle as accurately as you can near the bottom of the page to represent the front of the brick.

3 Draw a cross near one of the top corners of the page. This is the vanishing point.

4 Now, using your ruler, lightly draw perspective lines from each corner of the brick to the vanishing point.

5 Using the perspective lines as guides, draw in the sides of the brick.

Inside views

The purpose of a technical illustration of, say, a basketball shoe is to show its outer shape so that a range of people can see the designer's idea for its appearance. But some illustrations, for example of a car, may need to show the parts inside as well, such as the engine or the gears.

Illustrators use different ways to show the outside and inside at the same time. An **exploded view** shows the **component parts** moved from their actual positions, so they can be seen clearly. It provides a guide to how parts fit and work together. A **cutaway** is an illustration of the outside with a section of the surface cut away to reveal what is underneath. Therefore, only some of the inside parts are shown.

Designing with computers

Today, technical drawings and illustrations are usually created using computer-aided design (**CAD**). Sophisticated CAD software packages enable designers to accurately draw and illustrate everything from furniture to aeroplanes on-screen. Examples of CAD software include *AutoCAD*, *VariCAD*, and *Pro/Desktop*. To operate the software, CAD designers need a mouse, **light-pen**, or **digital tablet**.

This cutaway illustration of a space shuttle reveals both its outer shape and what is hidden away inside.

This designer is using a light-pen and digital tablet to amend a CAD scooter illustration on her monitor.

Just a tool

CAD takes a lot of the time-consuming work out of making technical drawings. On a computer it is easy to adjust things such as colour, shading, shape, and scale. If a design needs to be tweaked to get it right, it is a case of adjusting a small bit of CAD programming rather than completely redesigning and drawing a product. It also helps technical artists to express their ideas clearly and easily so others can understand them.

However, the technical illustrator still needs to know the basic principles of drawing. The computer is just a tool, and will only produce good design when operated by a creative user.

A different perspective

Adding perspective to a CAD drawing does not involve drawing perspective lines and vanishing points. CAD software allows a design to be viewed from any angle and at any scale with the push of a few buttons. Surface texture, colours, and light reflections can be added, so designers can produce very high-quality visualizations that look very much like the real thing.

It is easier to visualize designs, such as this intricate piping system for a new ship, by building accurate models.

Giving an idea a "form"

Three-dimensional design illustrations on-screen can look fantastic, but for many products the best way to spot design problems is to construct a model. This is especially important for objects that are going to be **mass-produced** in factories, such as toys, because it is expensive to buy the materials and set up machines to make them.

Design models need to be accurate. They should be constructed using technical drawings with dimensioning information. Models of small objects are often life-size, but large objects such as aeroplanes are made as **scale models**.

Sculpting and prototyping

Designers sculpt traditional design models from a variety of materials. For example, they may carve out shapes from blocks of foam or soft wood such as balsa, or construct models from cardboard or clay. These materials are used to create the outer shape of the object.

For some objects, models are constructed from the same materials as the final product. They may have working parts that are made either to scale or full-size. Working models like this are called **prototypes**. A prototype of a new car, for example, would have opening doors and a detailed interior to demonstrate the ergonomics.

CAD to CAM modelling

Today, some simple models are made automatically using computers. Special programs convert design information from a CAD program into information for producing the model of the product on a machine. This is computer-aided manufacture or **CAM**. Some CAM systems are attached to machines that cut away material such as plastic from a block to leave the model. Other systems build up layers of material one at a time to create a model of an object. This process is called stereolithography. This is how one type of stereolithography works:

● the designer creates a 3D model of an object on a computer using a CAD program

● CAM software "slices" the model up on-screen into about ten thin layers for each millimetre of the model

● a **laser system** shines a pattern of light in the shape of the first slice or layer on to a tank of special liquid plastic; the plastic hardens where the light reaches it, forming the first layer of the model

● a platform in the tank drops down a little, so the first layer is submerged

● the laser shines light down again to harden more liquid plastic in the shape of the second layer of the model

● this process is repeated, layer-by-layer, until the model is complete.

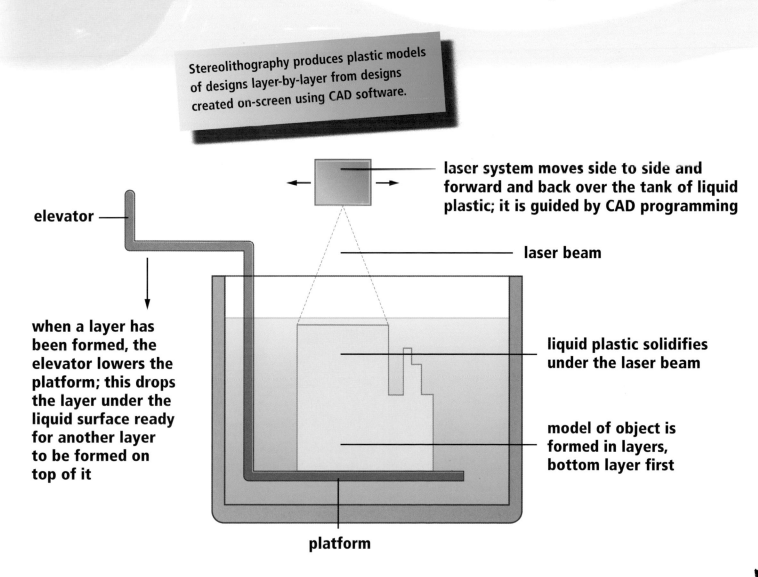

Stereolithography produces plastic models of designs layer-by-layer from designs created on-screen using CAD software.

elevator

when a layer has been formed, the elevator lowers the platform; this drops the layer under the liquid surface ready for another layer to be formed on top of it

laser system moves side to side and forward and back over the tank of liquid plastic; it is guided by CAD programming

laser beam

liquid plastic solidifies under the laser beam

model of object is formed in layers, bottom layer first

platform

Graphic design

Most products are embellished with **graphics** to make them more distinctive, memorable, or appealing to their target audience – the people who might buy them. Graphic designers use images, drawn and photographed, and lettering for graphics. They work mostly on-screen using software such as *Illustrator* and *Photoshop*. Graphic design is at the heart of the advertising, marketing, and publishing industries.

A bold logo such as this for Flip skateboards is clearly recognizable from a distance.

Logos

Logos are simple graphics that identify uniquely a company or its products. For example, a skateboard maker may design a distinctive logo and pay famous boarders to wear it on their clothing. They may also use the logo in adverts in boarding magazines or on hoardings at skateboard competitions. Customers may then buy boards with this logo on because they associate the brand with the famous boarders they have seen wearing the logo and believe they are using the best. Logos without words, such as the Nike "swoosh", are often quicker to recognize than those with words and can be understood anywhere in the world.

Graphic designers experiment with different fonts and arrangements of text and images to produce final designs.

The world of fonts

Look around a supermarket at food packages and you will see hundreds of fonts. A font is a particular way of writing letters. For example, the font used for these words is different from the font used for newspaper headlines. Some fonts are designed to be read easily over lots of lines, as in a novel. Others are designed to have an impact from a distance, as on the side of a racing car. Fonts may also be chosen to suit certain styles of text or to communicate information in different ways. For example, **Albertus** looks more serious than Lemonade and *handskript* looks more ancient than Skia.

Page design

As well as choosing appropriate fonts to present information, graphic designers also decide how words and images should be combined and laid out for best effect. For example, book designers decide how many lines there will be on a page and how blocks of text and images should be combined. They design pages in books for young children with larger lettering and fewer words than on pages in adult books.

Try it yourself

Imagine your favourite band is losing popularity. They have come to you to design a new look to help them appeal to a wider audience. Come up with three designs of your own for a CD case for their music, using computer software such as *Microsoft Publisher*. Use different fonts and images, drawn or scanned in, and vary the **composition**, by having images in different positions or sizes on the cover.

objects of design

Some designs, such as a flash new mobile phone, get noticed immediately. But the designs of many of the everyday objects we use and take for granted – from pens and chairs to televisions and bottles – are also the result of careful, innovative design.

The chair

Two hundred years ago, all chairs were designed by craftsmen from different types of solid wood. Wood is a durable, hard material that is easy to work with, using simple tools. Since then, new production techniques have emerged allowing wood to be shaped using machines. For example, in 1859 Michael Thonet invented a process for machine-forming rods of **laminated** wood and then curving and bending them using high-pressure steam to create new chair shapes. Designers have access to many different materials for chairs today including plastics, metals, and glass. However, wood still remains popular because its all-round properties are hard to beat.

The write stuff

Have you ever tried to write with one of those enormous novelty pencils? It is tricky because it is difficult to balance and control the pencil. Almost all writing and drawing instruments measure about 14–17 centimetres (5.5–6.5 inches) long because this is a comfortable ergonomic length. Wooden pencils and ball-point pens are commonly hexagonal for good grip and less than 1 centimetre (0.5 inches) wide. These standard measurements are used in the design of desk tidies, pencil cases, and stationery slots in rucksacks.

Mass innovators

Some designers create objects that become so widely used that they take on the designer's name. For example, the ball-point pen was invented by the Hungarian journalist Laszlo Biro in 1938. Impressed by how quick-drying the ink used on newspapers was, he tried it in his fountain pen. It clogged up the nib. So, with his brother's help, Biro invented a tubular nib with a metal ball at the tip that rolled to let the ink out gradually. Their new, mass-produced ball-points soon became known as biros.

Designer focus: Philippe Starck

The French designer Philippe Starck designs anything from buildings, furniture, and luggage, to noodles, toothbrushes, and spectacle frames. He is one of the most famous designers in the world. Starck used to make a lot of designer objects, with up-to-the-minute style. However, his more recent designs have been created to be durable and last a long time, rather than "throw away" things that only survive for as long as they remain in fashion.

Arne Jacobsen created these chair designs out of laminated wood in the 1950s. Today's versions have the same design, but they are often coated in bright, modern colours.

Technology-led designs

If you go to your local library or film rental shop you will have noticed that there are far fewer videos around than there used to be. The video cassette, a plastic box containing a reel of magnetic tape, is being replaced by DVDs (digital video discs). These discs store films and other audiovisual information in a compact digital, high-definition format.

The shape of a DVD is simple, but it has had a big effect on the design of many related items. For example, DVD boxes are thinner with less space on the spine for graphics than a video cassette box. DVD players and recorders are much smaller than video recorders. This is because the discs are smaller. Also, the device that reads information off the disc, a moving laser system, is more compact than the heads used to read the tape in a video. Changes in design like this, brought about by changing technology, are described as technology-led.

Game on

The realistic, virtual worlds of home video games today are completely different from the first games that appeared in the 1970s. The Atari Pong was the first widely available games **console**. It could play just one game, a sort of very simple table-tennis called Pong. The console was a big metal and wood-effect plastic box that was plugged into a television. It was controlled by two knobs on the front.

Designers soon began to create consoles that users could play different games on by slotting in different cartridges or discs. They designed game controllers that were separate from the consoles and had different buttons to control different aspects of the games. They also designed consoles with slots for different controllers for multiplayer gaming.

As more and more people began to play games against others over the Internet, designers created consoles that could be used online. Many of these included built-in memories, so players could resume games from the point they had reached and saved, rather than starting again each time.

Home screens

The televisions we view DVDs on all used to be heavy, bulky CRT (cathode ray tube) monitors, but today other designs are available with thinner, lighter LCD (liquid crystal display) screens. These new technology-led television designs have developed from screens used on laptop computers. Some people buy LCD televisions because they save space and are slightly clearer to watch, but many buy them because they make their homes look more modern.

Today's consoles, such as the Xbox 360, look very sleek and modern compared with Pong, but their external design is still influenced by what is inside.

Xbox 360 console ————

Going out, getting smaller

In the 1960s a single computer much less powerful than those in your school or home would occupy a whole room. Music players, calculators, digital cameras, and mobile phones have also become smaller since they were first invented. The change in size is driven partly by changes in technology and partly by changing consumer demand.

People want portable devices because they are travelling more than before and they want things that are easier to carry. The first Walkman, Sony's portable cassette player, weighed 400 grams (14 ounces), the weight of a tin of tomatoes. The latest Walkman mp3 players weigh a quarter of this and can store thousands of tracks.

Designer focus: Jonathan Ive

Jonathan Ive is one of the most famous designers in the world. His use of coloured and translucent plastics has influenced many other designers. He says, "As a kid, I remember taking apart whatever I could get my hands on. Later, this developed into more of an interest in how they were made, how they worked, their form and material." He helped design a new-looking computer, the iMac, for the Apple computer company, which sold in great numbers. Later, Ive created the iPod mp3 player, the first popular mp3 player.

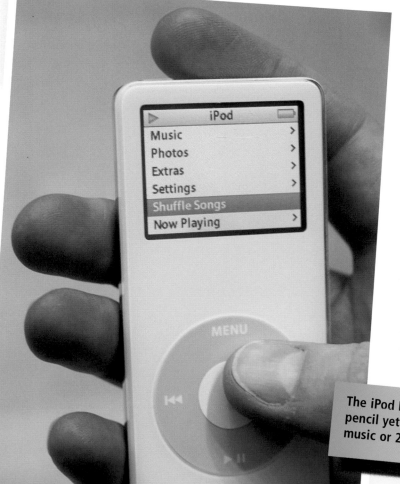

Keeping in touch

The first mobile phones weighed about 20 kilograms (44 pounds) so they were hardly portable. Today, many mobile phones weigh less than 100 grams (4 ounces). New, miniaturized technology, such as small LCD screens, aerials, and loudspeakers, and more powerful small batteries have allowed designers to reduce the size of mobiles since they first appeared in the late 1980s. There has been rapid growth in global wireless networks and technology so that users can send messages cheaply across the planet. They use mobiles not only to send calls, texts, music, photos, and videos, but also to access websites.

The iPod Nano is the thickness of a pencil yet can store 3 days' worth of music or 25,000 photos.

A design team at the Samsung headquarters in Seoul, South Korea, discusses material, colours, and finishes for a new range of mobile phones.

Try it yourself

Your task is to design two mobile phones – one for a teenager and one for a seven-year-old child. Each should have an emergency "call home" button. Draw them accurately using a sharp pencil on smooth paper. Remember to think about the function and form of the phones, as well as the needs of the user. Think carefully about how the colour, shape, and fonts or images used on each could be different. Here are some ergonomic design tips:

● button size – young children usually have smaller hands than teenagers

● lettering and numbering – young children cannot read as well as teenagers

● durability and safety – young children may drop or forget the mobile phone.

New processes

The design of new, sleek, miniature gadgets has been possible partly because of new industrial processes. In the past, different types of plastic were rarely mixed together. Today it is possible to mould together different plastics and even plastic and metal. This is called **twin shooting**. It allows designers to make things in new ways out of plastic.

The iPod is made from twin-shot plastic whose outer layer looks delicate yet is strengthened by a tougher inner layer. It was designed as a tough sealed unit with no fasteners and no battery doors. New processes that will drive future design include the use of adhesives and lasers to join different metals.

Packaged up

For a designer, packaging has to do three things – protect, preserve, and identify a product. The clear box containing cherry tomatoes in a supermarket stops the fruit being squashed, is clear so customers can see what is inside, and has holes so air can circulate to stop the tomatoes going mouldy. Some packaging, such as a plastic bottle of bleach or medicine, needs special lids to stop children opening them because what is inside could be harmful.

Responsible design

Discarded goods and packaging cause pollution. Toxic metals used in computers, televisions, and other gadgets ooze into landfill sites and non-biodegradable packaging piles up. Designers of computers and cars, for example, can make a difference by creating products that are easy to recycle when they are finished with.

Recycled materials

Increased recycling worldwide is producing new recycled materials for designers to make things from. Recycled plastic is cheaper but has an uneven colour and texture compared to new plastic. Some designers use twin shooting to hide recycled plastic. For example, part of a chair could be made in tough, black recycled plastic but then skimmed with a rubbery, coloured plastic so it looks and feels better.

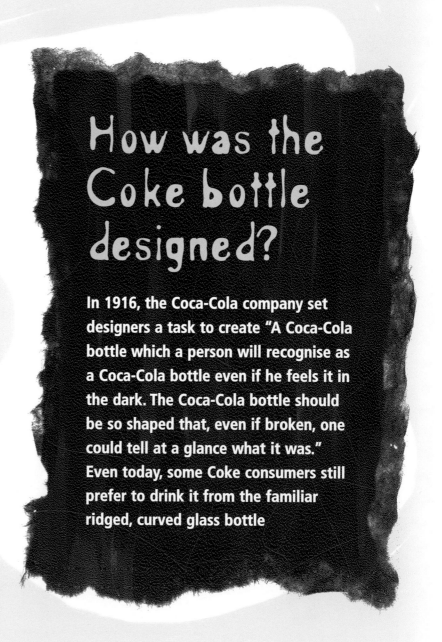

How was the Coke bottle designed?

In 1916, the Coca-Cola company set designers a task to create "A Coca-Cola bottle which a person will recognise as a Coca-Cola bottle even if he feels it in the dark. The Coca-Cola bottle should be so shaped that, even if broken, one could tell at a glance what it was." Even today, some Coke consumers still prefer to drink it from the familiar ridged, curved glass bottle

The Coca-Cola glass bottle is one of the most easily recognized containers in the world.

Designing for the web

Web design is a branch of design that expanded massively during the 1990s. Today, most businesses and many individuals have websites selling their products or telling the world about themselves. A good web design helps readers get to the information they need from the different pages on a website.

It is fairly easy to design a simple website using a web editor program, such as *Claris Home Page* or *Adobe Page Mill*. However, it is useful to practise a bit of **HTML**, or HyperText Mark-up Language, which is the universal language of the web. When you look at any website using a **browser** such as Internet Explorer or Netscape, you are actually looking at HTML files. The words are surrounded by coding that describes, in computer language, how they will be presented on a web page.

1 Go into your computer's list of built-in programs and find NotePad (on a PC) or TextEdit or SimpleText (on a Mac). These are text editor programs.

2 Type in <HTML> on the first line, hit return, and type "This is my website." Hit return and type </HTML>. The coding marks the top and bottom of your web page, so everything you put on your page goes in-between.

3 Save the file in a folder you can find easily and name it "designtest1.html". (If you are using TextEdit, you will need to format your document as plain text using the plain text option from the format menu.)

4 You can now open your Internet browser and browse the folders until you find "designtest1.html" to see your web page.

5 Now go back into the text editor and add some more text to "designtest1.html". Between "This is my website." and "</HTML>", type in "I want to be a web designer."

6 Now add a line space before and after this line. You can do this by typing in <P> and </P> below the line.

7 Make the word "web" bold by typing <B> before and </B> after it.

8 You can add pictures, too. Create a simple logo in Paint or other drawing software. Save the file as "mylogo.gif" in the same folder as the HTML file. Decide where you want the picture on the page and type in: <IMG SRC="mylogo.gif">.

9 Now add a link to a favourite website. Type "One day I might get as good as the designer of my <A HREF="www.???">favourite</A> website!". (Insert your favourite website's address instead of the question marks.)

10 Finally, make your text look different by positioning it in the centre of the page. You can do this by typing <CENTER> before the first line of text and </CENTER> after the last line of text.

11 Save everything you have done and view your web page in your browser.

```
<HTML>
<CENTER>
This is my website.
<P>
I want to be a <B>web</B> designer.
</P>
<IMG SRC="mylogo.gif">
One day I might get as good as the
designer of my
<A HREF="www.???">favourite</A> website!
</CENTER>
</HTML>
```

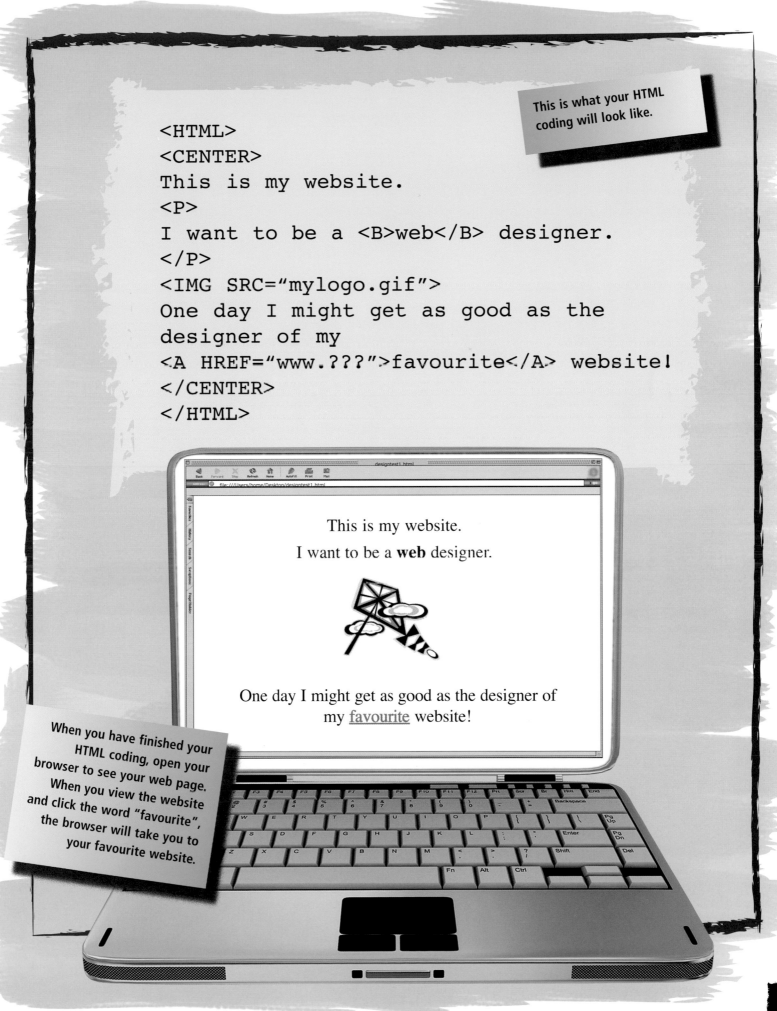

When you have finished your HTML coding, open your browser to see your web page. When you view the website and click the word "favourite", the browser will take you to your favourite website.

Design on the skyline

Look across a city and the skyline is crammed with different shaped buildings. The structures in and amongst which we live, work, and study are designed by architects.

Creating buildings

Like other designers, architects start the design process by considering some basic questions such as what the building is for, how many people will use it, and what activities will take place in the building. The answers to these questions will affect the design.

A building's form

As well as thinking about the building's function, the architect must also consider its form and how it will fit in with the buildings around it.

On a new housing estate, architects may design lots of similar buildings that will blend together and look unified. However, in a built-up city buildings may either be designed to blend in with or to be very different from the surrounding buildings.

Material world

Architects also need to decide which materials to use. Strong materials such as reinforced concrete are used to support buildings, but these materials may be clad or hidden behind other materials, such as brick or glass. Some materials used on the outside of a building change with time. For example, wood may bleach and steel may rust.

Many architects are designing **green buildings**, which use renewable materials and cause as little pollution as possible. These buildings are also designed to be energy efficient. For example, they may have triple-glazed windows to let in natural light and trap heat.

Plans and models

Most architects draw detailed dimensioned drawings of their designs. There may be a different plan for each storey of a building and illustrations of views from different directions. Buildings are very expensive to make so architects make accurate scale models to help clients visualize designs.

Traditionally, architects make **blueprints**. These are copies of plans with white lines on blue paper. Constructors and engineers use the blueprints to work from. Many architects today design on-screen using 3D software. This allows them to create virtual models of their buildings which clients can "visit".

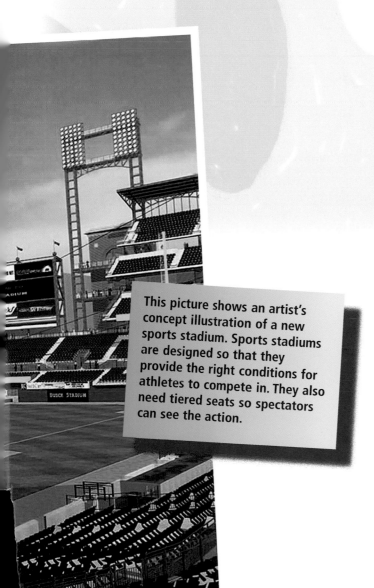

This picture shows an artist's concept illustration of a new sports stadium. Sports stadiums are designed so that they provide the right conditions for athletes to compete in. They also need tiered seats so spectators can see the action.

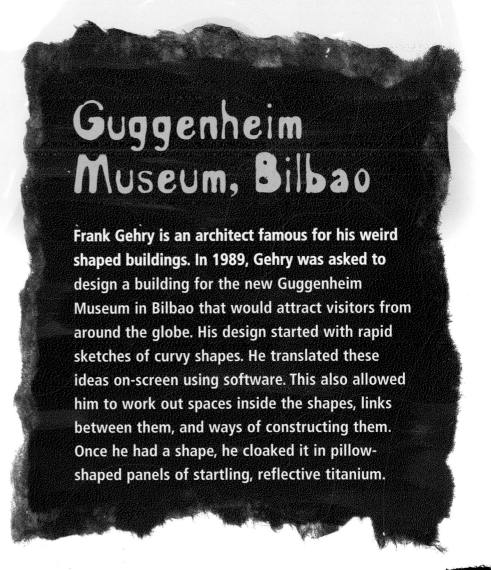

Guggenheim Museum, Bilbao

Frank Gehry is an architect famous for his weird shaped buildings. In 1989, Gehry was asked to design a building for the new Guggenheim Museum in Bilbao that would attract visitors from around the globe. His design started with rapid sketches of curvy shapes. He translated these ideas on-screen using software. This also allowed him to work out spaces inside the shapes, links between them, and ways of constructing them. Once he had a shape, he cloaked it in pillow-shaped panels of startling, reflective titanium.

Architects can use 3D computer software to illustrate how a skyscraper will look next to other buildings. This computer-generated design illustration shows how the new Freedom Tower, to be built in New York City, will look once it is completed.

Going up

Very tall buildings can be visually impressive. They also hold more people than low-rise buildings, so they are often built in highly populated areas where land is scarce or expensive, as in New York City.

The first skyscrapers appeared in the late 19th century. These buildings were designed with an internal steel skeleton and an outer skin of brick or glass. The weight of the building was supported by the steel skeleton rather than load-bearing brick walls, as in normal buildings.

Reducing shear

Taller, heavier buildings are less rigid than lower, lighter buildings. Earthquakes and strong winds can make them shear, or sway from side to side. Too much shear and they may collapse. When architects design skyscrapers, they need to reduce shear. They may fit enormous shock absorbers between floors or design them to be built on flexible **foundations**.

Mind the gap

The first bridges in history probably consisted of fallen tree trunks or slabs of stone spanning the gap between the two banks of a stream or river. These were a simple type of beam bridge. Beam bridges consist of a rigid beam supported at either end by something hard such as rock or a brick pillar. Beam bridges are limited in length to less than 80 metres (250 feet). Any longer than that and they collapse owing to the weight pulling downwards on the beam.

To span really wide gaps, architects need to link together lots of shorter beam bridges or choose other designs. Suspension bridges can be built across very wide spans. In a suspension bridge, the beam is suspended from long cables which hang between towers at either end. The ends of the cables are anchored to the ground on either side of the span.

Cable-stayed bridges look quite similar to suspension bridges, but the cables supporting the beam or deck are attached directly to tall towers.

Try it yourself

Try this exercise to test the strength of two bridge designs. You will need six bricks and a piece of string about 1.5 metres (5 feet) long.

Stand two bricks upright on the floor so they are about 50 centimetres (20 inches) apart and tie the string tightly around their tops. When you push down on the string, the bricks collapse inwards. Now repeat the test with the string loosely hanging over the top of the bricks and anchored to the ground at either end with a pile of two bricks. This time the bricks should remain upright when you push on the string.

What's inside counts

Architects plan how spaces will be used in general, but **interior designers** work out in detail how spaces should be divided up, lit, furnished, and decorated. In a clothes shop, for example, they design everything from the arrangement of spotlights and mirrors in changing rooms to the materials used for chairs and curtains.

For an office, interior designers work out the best way to fit in enough desks for all the workers and create partitions and walls so workers with different jobs do not interrupt each other. For a classroom used by very young children, designers specify smaller chairs and tables than those used by older children.

Anthropometrics

Interior designers use detailed information about the size of the human body so they know how much space people need. This is called **anthropometrics**.

Anthropometrics is used in all kinds of interior design. For example, designers use information about how much space people need when they design kitchens. They need to make sure the space in front of a cooker is big enough. It must be possible for someone to open the door and get food out of the oven without banging their back against cupboards.

Mind the traffic

Interior designers also consider **traffic throughflow** – the ways people usually move through and use spaces.

Examining traffic throughflow helps designers decide on where to position things. For example, it is better to position chairs and tables around the edge of a café, where people can look out of the window. If tables and chairs are put near the entrance to the café or near the counter, they get in the way of people coming in or out of the café and of customers ordering their food and drinks.

Try it yourself

What furniture would you ideally have in your bedroom? Apart from a bed and desk, maybe you need space for a drum kit and a pet cage?

Measure the width of the walls, doors, and windows of your bedroom and draw an accurate plan of it, to scale, on graph paper. Then cut out pieces of paper in the shapes of the furniture you want to go in it, also to scale. Now design a room layout by trying the pieces in different positions within the room, remembering to think about anthropometrics and traffic throughflow.

Once you are happy with the design, why not try to illustrate your bedroom from different angles, using perspective?

Designers used traffic throughflow data in order to create this design for a shopping complex with underground train station under a curved glass roof.

33

Design on the move

The major reason we use cars, aeroplanes, trains, and boats is to help us get from "A" to "B". But there are many factors influencing the design of new vehicles, including speed, style, safety, convenience, and cost.

Car design

All cars are pretty similar. They are oblong vehicles with a wheel near each corner, an engine, and a cabin for the driver, passengers, and luggage. But they vary in size and style, from a Smart car to a Ferrari. Some, such as MPVs (multi-purpose vehicles), put more emphasis on carrying people and loads, while others, such as sports coupes, concentrate on speed and luxury.

The vehicle specification

The first step in the car design process is to decide upon the vehicle **specification**. The specification lists details of the car's features and includes some of the following information:

● the size of the car, including its height, width, length, and weight

● exterior details, including the number of doors, the style of the exterior, and the materials used for the body panels

● engine details, including its size and the power it can produce.

This designer is using a bank of computer equipment to turn a concept illustration into finished 3D CAD images of a new Renault car.

You can see the 2D drawing and 3D illustration used as reference in creating this full-size clay model.

Concept designs

The next step for car designers is to brainstorm ideas and come up with concept sketches based on the vehicle specification. Today, most concepts are made up into 3D CAD images. Many are shown to members of the public to see whether they would be interested in buying such a car. Their comments may be used to modify the design. Once the concept designs are agreed upon, designers can move on to modelling.

Clay models

Car designers commonly make full-size clay models of their concepts. First a light but solid foam core, roughly in the shape of the car, is made. Then modelling clay is applied to this foam core. The clay is added bit by bit to match the dimensions and curves shown on the technical drawings and illustrations. Designers need sculpting skills to shape and smooth the clay to make the model accurate.

Concept design to final car

Once a clay model of a new vehicle has been completed and the design has been agreed upon, a full prototype is made showing the detail of both the interior and exterior parts. Mechanics and engineers work with designers to make sure that working parts operate properly. They also work out ways in which new components needed for the prototype can best be made in factories. Finally, once everything has been checked, the new car may be put into production.

Crash tests

All newly designed vehicles go through a series of tests. These include crash tests and test drives. In crash tests, people-sized models called crash dummies are belted into the car and the car is pushed hard into a solid wall. The test is filmed and measurements are taken, showing how the car and its passengers are affected by a crash. This is a way of testing the safety and strength of the car.

Test driving

Test driving a car reveals whether it works properly when actually being used. Sometimes this may reveal problems in the design. For example, the first production Mercedes A-class cars toppled over when driven fast around corners! As a result of this, Mercedes had to change the design to make it safer to drive.

The graphic on the crash dummy's head helps testers examine how well seat belts perform in new car designs.

Concept cars

A concept car is a one-off prototype developed from a designer's concept design. Car manufacturers make concept cars to show off their design skills and hint at the fantastic cars they may make in the future.

Some of the new ideas seen in concept cars may later appear in the cars we can buy. For example, the computerized sensors to help judge parking distances found on some cars today started life as an idea on a concept car. Here are some examples of ideas on recent concept cars that may appear in the future:

- Saab Aero X – a car with no doors! The windscreen and side windows are one piece of glass. This and the roof form a canopy that lifts up as one unit.

- Jeep Treo – a car with no engine designed to be powered by small fuel cells that should be possible in the future. It has built-in bike racks!

- Dodge Polycar – a car made of plastics so it is light.

- Renault Egeus – a car with seats that swivel outwards to make getting in easier and flush-fitting door handles that spring out when a person's hand comes near to them.

The innovative Saab Aero X concept car has a totally new kind of roof that lifts up.

Urban transporters

Many designers have created new ways of transporting people individually around cities. Small vehicles, such as mopeds, are easier to manoeuvre and park, and cheaper to run than cars. Most small vehicles are designed to run on roads, but the Segway was designed to travel on pedestrian routes. The designer Dean Kamen developed the Segway from a self-balancing wheelchair that can climb stairs. Computers and motors in the base keep the Segway upright at all times. Users lean forwards to move forwards, and backwards to move backwards. Kamen imagined his design could make walking a thing of the past, but its high cost and limited use for getting around cities built around roads has made it less popular than he hoped.

Sustainable cars

Today, most people acknowledge that oil is running out and that burning fuel in cars and other vehicles contributes to global warming and pollution. Scientists and engineers are developing new, sustainable power sources. These include oil alternatives such as biodiesel, made from vegetable oil, and solar cells, which convert sunlight into electricity.

New power sources create challenges for designers. For example, at present only very light, experimental cars have been designed that run efficiently on solar power, and they only work in places that get a lot of strong sunlight. Most car roofs are too small to fit in sufficient solar cells to provide enough power to run the car and the cells are very expensive. Future solar cell technology and designs may make solar-powered cars more widespread.

A group of tourists use Segways in front of the White House during a sightseeing tour of Washington DC.

This experimental solar car has panels on its roof that convert sunlight into electricity to power the car's battery.

Try it yourself

Why not try this mountainboard project? You can find details of a website where you can find information about mountainboards on page 54 of this book.

1 Research typical mountainboard dimensions and designs on the web.

2 How are the trucks (the metal bits with the wheels on), wheels, and decks shaped differently from those used on normal skateboards? What features help the rider to stay on when the going gets bumpy?

3 Write down ideas for your own design. How could you make a better mountainboard? How about adding suspension or enclosing the front to protect the rider's legs? What materials would be best?

4 Draw your own design in top, bottom, and side views. Add dimensioning and show what scale you are drawing it at.

5 Now make a prototype. Ideally you may be able to get an old skateboard and customize it with different wheels, borrowed from an old toy or construction kit such as Lego Technic. Alternatively, make a smaller model of the board out of scrap wood, metal, cardboard, or plastic.

6 Finally, think how you would design an eye-catching logo for your board.

Fast trains

The design specification for most trains has been fairly similar since trains were first built over 200 years ago. However, many of today's trains travel faster than ever before, making it quicker to travel by train to some destinations than by aeroplane.

High-speed specifications

Building a faster train is not just a case of putting in a bigger engine. Designers of high-speed trains need to specify more powerful brakes than those on normal trains. They also need to specify special suspension systems to stop the train vibrating as it moves at high speed. High-speed trains are designed with streamlined locomotive fronts to prevent air **drag** and loud noise as the trains move along.

Staying on the tracks

Today's fastest high-speed trains, such as the bullet train, can travel at over 500 kmph (300 mph), but these speeds are only possible on long sections of straight track. If there are sharp curves, passengers get uncomfortable in their seats, things fly off tables owing to sideways forces, and trains may even come off the track. Many countries, including France and Japan, have created new, straight rail networks for their high-speed trains.

Designers in the United Kingdom have developed tilting trains that can "lean into curves" to reduce passenger discomfort at speed on the existing, curving tracks.

Different train carriages

The interiors of trains such as underground trains are designed differently from the interiors of long-distance, high-speed trains. Designers of underground trains generally place seats facing inwards in long rows down either side of the carriages. They leave plenty of space between the seats so the trains can accommodate standing passengers and people can easily get on and off.

Long-distance carriages are designed with more luxurious seats so that travellers will remain comfortable for longer. The seats are usually arranged in rows of two or three on either side of the carriage. Some carriages may have tables and even Internet connection points so that people can work as they travel.

New train design

The fastest trains in the world have been designed with no wheels! Maglev trains are designed to glide above a special track using the force of magnetic fields. They can go faster than trains with wheels because there is no friction between train and track slowing them down. Maglev trains cannot be used on existing railway tracks. This is because the tracks cannot be adapted easily to provide suitable magnetic fields to lift the train and keep it stable as it moves along. Therefore, designers need to create complete train systems including both carriages and track. This is one reason maglev projects are very expensive to build.

A maglev train, such as this one in Shanghai, China, is not slowed by friction, like normal trains, because no part of it touches the guide track.

Designing for flight

As in all design, the design of an aircraft depends on its function. The most basic function of all aeroplanes is to stay in the air and transport people or goods from one place to another. But aeronautic or aeroplane designers create many different types of aeroplane for different purposes, from tiny microlights and private jets to large passenger aircraft and military transport planes.

Wing design

One of the major choices in the design process for an aircraft is the type of wing. The shape of the wing affects how fast an aircraft can travel. There are two basic designs – triangular-shaped delta wings or rectangular wings.

Aircraft wings are thicker at the front than at the back and they are curved on top and flatter underneath. This shape is called an **aerofoil**. Air moving over the aerofoil creates lift. Big wings create more lift than small wings but also more drag or air resistance, which slows down the aeroplane.

Rectangular wings give enough lift for low-speed flying. Designers use large rectangular wings on slow, heavy transporter and passenger aeroplanes. They use short rectangular wings on small aircraft such as stunt aircraft.

Delta wings allow aircraft to fly at very high speeds. However, they create high drag when changing direction quickly. Designers use delta wings on very fast aircraft, such as jet fighters.

Aeroplane designers test the effects of body and wing shape on drag.

This computer-generated artwork shows the design for the X-43C, planned to be in the air in 2008. It will feature a new engine design that should allow it to fly at five times the speed of sound.

The X factor

New designs of aeroplanes are put to the test on the ground before they are made into prototypes. Designers place models of aeroplanes in wind tunnels or run sophisticated 3D modelling software to visualize drag and lift. However, new aeroplanes have to be flown to see how they perform when airborne.

In the United States there has been a programme of testing experimental aeroplane prototypes, or X-planes, since 1945. Different X-plane designs have included everything from vertical take-off and landing engines, to new light body materials such as carbon fibre.

Designers use technology from X-planes to make production aircraft. The new F-35 joint strike fighter, which will be a major international military aeroplane from 2008, was developed from the X-35.

Weight calculations

When aeronautic designers develop any aeroplane, they need to consider its total weight, not just the weight of the materials used to make its body. The heavier an aeroplane is, the more thrust it needs to stay airborne. For example, long-range airliners carry lots of heavy fuel to take passengers and their luggage great distances. Airliners have limits on the amount of luggage passengers can take on board because their wing and engine sizes are designed only to keep a certain weight in the air.

Inside aeroplanes

The design of the inside of an X-plane or a fighter jet looks rather basic in comparison to a large passenger aeroplane. The only things visible around the pilot and passenger are usually the instruments for flying the plane or communicating with air traffic controllers on the ground. Seats are basic but provide support while flying the aircraft and they can eject the occupants from the aeroplane if it is about to crash.

For airliners and private jets, interior designers create more comfortable surroundings for passengers. Each passenger has an adjustable seat. Designers incorporate fold-down tables into the back of seats and sometimes they have inbuilt television screens. They create overhead units that store luggage safely out of the way. Designers use anthropometrics to finalize the dimensions not only of each passenger's seating environment, but also many other aspects of the interior, from the size of onboard toilets to the width of food trolleys.

Outside influences

The future of aeroplane design will be affected by various factors. For example, if airlines have to pay to clean up the air pollution their aeroplanes cause in future, they are more likely to create fuel-saving airliners. Many aeroplane companies are already designing smaller, lighter airliners that can travel further on less fuel, whereas others are creating giants, such as the Airbus A380, that can transport more people per trip than existing aeroplanes.

Try it yourself

Why not try designing some paper planes with different wing shapes? Then test how far they can fly and how long they stay in the air. See some possible designs at www.workman.com//fliersclub/download.html. Choose your best planes and challenge some friends to develop a competing squadron.

Some passengers in airliners such as the Airbus A380 travel in mini-lounges. The seats allow passengers to stretch their legs and some are designed to turn into wide, comfortable beds.

Kit aeroplane

Aeroplanes are made up of many thousands of designed parts. If the parts do not fit together accurately when the aeroplane is assembled, their measurements have to be corrected, which wastes time and money. Parts for the Boeing 787 Dreamliner, which will fly from 2007, were designed on a CAD/CAM system by different teams. Designers then assembled a virtual Dreamliner on-screen, found out about any parts that did not fit and then adjusted the parts before the aircraft was actually assembled. By adjusting part designs in this way they reduced any error in fit to at most the thickness of a playing card. This error is far less than the previous industry standard of 10 millimetres (0.5 inches).

Creating boats and ships

The most important aspect of designing any ship or boat is **buoyancy**. Buoyancy is the upward force that keeps things afloat. A boat floats if it weighs the same or less than the water its **hull** displaces (pushes aside). Boat designers use light, strong materials such as fibreglass and carbon fibre to create small boats, such as rowing boats. The heaviest boats in the world, including supertankers and aircraft carriers, have enormous flat-bottomed steel hulls. They cannot move fast or change direction easily, but they remain afloat because they displace enough water. The weight of the water they displace is greater than the combined weight of their hulls and cargo plus the large air spaces within them.

Built for speed

For racing boats, maintaining speed while remaining stable and manoeuvrable is the highest priority.

For fast yachts, designers create computer systems to control the shape of sails depending on wind direction and speed. This ensures that the wind is pushing the yacht as fast as possible in all conditions.

As boats travel faster through water, they experience more drag. Designers reduce drag by creating narrow, streamlined hulls that do not sit low in the water. This can make fast boats unstable so they roll from side to side in waves or wind. Boat designers can add long underwater fins, called keels, or attach stabilizing wings to either side to help stabilize single hulls. They can also design fast boats such as catamarans, which are made of two narrow hulls linked together.

Boat designers may also use hydrofoils. These are horizontal wing-like structures attached to struts on a boat's underside. When the boat moves fast, water pushes the hydrofoils up, making the hull rise completely above the water.

Design difficulties

In 2000 a revolutionary new catamaran design took to the water. *Team Philips* was 27 metres (120 feet) long, 21 metres (70 feet) wide, and it had twin masts 41 metres high (135 feet). It was the world's largest carbon fibre structure. It was designed to beat round-the-world speed sailing records, but during sea trials, it snapped in two.

Designer Adrian Thompson blamed the way his design had actually been constructed into the finished boat. He found that a weight-bearing carbon strip inside the hull had not stuck correctly to the material around it. Others blamed the cutting-edge design, saying that it was not able to cope with conditions in the real ocean. Now the wreckage of the boat lies in a museum but other boat designers may learn from its design mistakes.

This is a prototype of the Dolphin personal water craft. The design brief was to create a boat that can ride on, leap out of, and dive under the water surface, rather like a real dolphin, with a reasonable price.

Going further

Do you plaster your bedroom walls with car posters? Have you ever doodled new inventions on bits of paper? Are you interested in the ergonomics of kitchen equipment? If so, then you may be the right sort of person to study design.

Improving your technical art

You probably already like to draw and model things, but if you want to be a technical artist you will have to develop your skills. There are many ways you can do this. For example, study the shapes of some handheld tools, such as a hammer or an electric drill, in detail.

Think about how each tool's form is affected by its function and by ergonomics. Measure and draw the objects accurately, to scale, with dimensioning.

You could also make some cardboard scale models of buildings. It could be something local, such as your house or a multistorey car park, or a famous building like the Sydney Opera House. Try to make your models neat by concealing the glue or sticky tape you use to assemble them.

The only way to get better at design and technical art is to practise!

A wide outlook

Designers get their ideas from many sources and they are influenced by all kinds of things around them. It is a good idea to carry a sketchbook with you so if you see a design you like, such as a T-shirt logo or the curves of a car, you can draw it. Study the work of different designers, artists, and architects using library books and museum displays. When you visit cinemas, shops, and other public buildings, think about how the spaces are planned, how they are furnished, and decorated, and how things are positioned so people can easily move through and use the spaces.

Studying other designers through history, you will notice trends. For example, designs from the 1930s, from clothes to posters, are different from designs of the 1970s. Events taking place in society can affect design, so follow current affairs. Try to find out about any new technologies, laws, materials, or fuels that might affect design in the future.

Some schools have CAD equipment enabling pupils to practise design on-screen.

Design at school

Most schools and colleges teach design. You may have the opportunity to design things such as printed fabrics, desk tidies, or mirror surrounds. You may be able to practise using CAD/CAM to make simple objects such as keyrings or candlesticks. There may also be lunchtime or after-school clubs for keen designers. When it is time to do some work experience, how about helping out an architect or other designer?

Art is not enough

Art and design both influence and are influenced by many other fields of study, such as maths, science, psychology, and music. Biology can be useful in understanding ergonomics and maths helps you work out the angles, scale, and dimensioning of a design. History can help explain why designs have changed over time. If you are serious about getting into design, keep up your studies in a whole range of subjects!

Building a portfolio

Your design portfolio has a simple purpose: to show others how good you are at designing. It should contain your best and most recent work, so you have to keep it up to date. The portfolio has to demonstrate that you can draw and model, so put in originals or photos of what you have achieved. As well as complete designs, you can include any design exercises you may have done, such as any "Try it yourself" exercises that you have tried from this book.

Your portfolio should also show that you can think like a designer. It should demonstrate that you can come up with original ideas but also know how to turn them into designs that could work.

It is a good idea to include in your portfolio some design ideas that you did not choose. Show the reasons why you rejected the ideas. This will show others that you understand how factors such as anthropometrics, ergonomics, and suitability of materials affect design.

Prove your design skills by putting together an imaginative, varied, and tidy portfolio.

Gradual specialization

After you have studied art and design at school, the next step is college. Most colleges offer general art and design courses for new students. They touch on lots of different types of design while also bringing the skills of new students up to scratch. Many students then move on to take more specialized design courses. Some will know exactly what they want to specialize in from the outset, but others will find that out as they study. The many specialized areas of design include fashion, automotive, interiors, graphics, gardens, theatre, model-making, multimedia, and textiles. The facilities at college, including powerful computers for 3D design and a wide range of materials for model-making, will allow you to turn your ideas into reality.

Architecture at college

Being an architect is not just about designing complete buildings but also about adding to or changing existing ones. This requires detailed knowledge about building techniques, planning laws, and building history. That is one reason why architecture courses are the longest of any designer, typically five years or more at college.

It may take years of training at college and in architectural firms, but one day you may have the chance to design and create buildings as distinctive as 30 St Mary Axe, popularly known as the "Gherkin" in London.

Glossary

2D having two dimensions – width and height. When something is 2D, it has no depth and looks flat.

3D having three dimensions – width, height, and depth. 3D is short for "three dimensional". When something is drawn to look 3D, it looks solid, not flat.

aerofoil wing shape that can produce lift in moving objects

anthropometrics measurement of the size, weight, and proportions of the human body

architect person who plans, designs, and often oversees the construction of buildings

blueprint in construction, design plan or technical drawing that contains a lot of detail about a building

brainstorming generating ideas amongst a group of people

browser in computing, program used to display HTML files used to navigate the Internet

buoyancy upward force on an object in liquid that makes the object float

CAD (computer-aided design) use of computer software to create accurate drawings, illustrations, and models of new design ideas

CAM (computer-aided manufacture) use of computer software to control the machinery in the manufacturing process

component part part or element of something, especially part of a machine or vehicle

composition arrangement of separate elements in a design or other illustration

concept design idea that is worked up into a design

console small machine designed to play video games

cutaway drawing or model representing something in which the outside is cut away to reveal the inner parts

digital tablet device consisting of a flat board and a light-pen used to enter designs directly into a computer by drawing them

dimensioning indicating the exact size and position of an object in a technical drawing

drag slowing force of water or air on something moving through them

ergonomics application of information about the needs of users to the design of equipment and environments so the design is easy and comfortable for people to use

exploded view illustration of an object in which its parts are displaced from their actual positions to show how they are put together

form the shape and appearance an object takes

foundations substructure that supports a building, usually hidden underground

friction resistance to motion between two surfaces in contact

function what something is used for

graphics images including pictures, photos, logos, and words that decorate and identify an object, product, or organization

green buildings buildings that are designed to be energy efficient and use renewable materials

HTML (HyperText Mark-up Language) computer language used to write web pages

hull frame or body of a boat or ship

illustration drawing that expresses an idea, but is not necessarily technically accurate

interior designer person who designs the furniture and decoration of the rooms inside a house or other building

laminated coated with a thin layer of plastic

laser system equipment that can precisely alter the position and strength of laser beams, which are powerful beams of light

light-pen light-sensitive device shaped like a pen, used to draw on a computer screen

magnetic field invisible lines of force surrounding a magnetic object

mass-produced produced in large numbers on a factory production line

perspective the way in which objects appear in relation to each other. Using the rules of perspective can make 2D illustrations appear 3D.

portfolio collection of a designer's creative work to show to potential employers and others

prototype full-scale working model used to test a design concept by making actual observations and necessary adjustments

scale ratio between the size of something and a representation of it

scale model representation of an object that is usually smaller than the actual size of that object

specification set of requirements for, or attributes of, an object

technical drawing exact scale or full-size drawing of an object, usually with details about size and position of its components

thrust force that pushes a plane forward. An engine provides the thrust for flight.

traffic throughflow way in which people usually move through and use a particular space

twin shooting method of moulding different plastics or plastic and metal together at the same time

vanishing point point on the horizon line at which parallel lines appear to meet

Find out more

Useful websites

Inspirational designs and designers

http://www.autozine.org/Styling/Styling.htm
The first of three pages showing famous car designers and their creations.

http://www.designmuseum.org/digital/
A virtual design museum.

http://www.greatbuildings.com
Take a virtual tour of some of the famous buildings of the world by downloading free 3D graphics. You will also have to download free viewing software called DesignWorkshop lite (http://www.artifice.com/dw_lite.html).

http://www.mbs.com
Information about mountainboard designs, protective gear, and photos of riders.

http://www.philippe-starck.com
The website of Philippe Starck, designer of anything from lamps and lemon squeezers to luggage and buildings. Contains lots of photos and some of his design illustrations.

http://www.wallpaper.com/design
The latest in designs of lots of different objects from bridges to glassware.

Drawing exercises

http://www.biro-art.com/
See what you could be drawing just using a biro!

http://www.ider.herts.ac.uk/school/
Click on 'Online courseware' for a good introduction to design, including exercises to improve your drawing skills.

http://itchstudios.com/psg/art_tut.htm
Useful art tutorial with lots on shading and showing reflections (here called radiosity).

http://www.lego.com/eng/factory/design/
Make some virtual Lego models.

http://www.olejarz.com/arted/perspective/
A site that introduces the principles of one-point perspective, with step-by-step instructions.

http://www.technologystudent.com
A graphic design site with lots of exercises for drawing and design practice.

General design

www.design-council.org.uk
Website of the Design Council, an organization that promotes the role of design and aims to ensure that designers and students of design have the right skills.

http://www.design-technology.info
A website designed for students of technology and anyone interested in products and design. Includes lots of information about well-known designers and their designs.

http://www.baddesigns.com/examples.html
An excellent site that includes lots of examples of things that are badly designed, from the arrangement of traffic lights above busy junctions to easily confused packaging graphics. The site also includes suggestions on how to improve the designs.

Books

Amazing Machines (Design Challenge series), by Keith Good (Evans Brothers, 2003)

The Big Book of Illustration Ideas, by Roger Walton (HarperCollins, 2004)

Dave's Quick 'n' Easy Web Pages: An Introductory Guide to Creating Web Sites, by Dave Lindsay (Erin Publications, 2001)

Design Drawing, by Francis Ching (Warner Books, 1997)

Drawing for Dummies, by Brenda Hoddinott (Hungry Minds Inc., 2003)

How Cool Stuff Works, by Chris Woodford and Ben Morgan (Dorling Kindersley, 2005)

Manual of Illustration Techniques, by Catharine Slade (A&C Black, 2003)

Pencil Sketching, by Thomas Wang (John Wiley, 2001)

Sketching and Drawing: An Easy Guide to Drawing for Beginners (No Experience Required series), by Larry Blovits (North Light Books, 2004)

Skyscrapers: Super Structures to Design and Build (Kaleidoscope Kids series) by Carol A. Johmann (Williamson Publishing, 2001)

Super Structures (Design Challenge series), by Keith Good (Evans Brothers, 2003)

Taking it further – courses

http://arc.co.uk/schools.arx
A list of art and design schools and colleges in the United Kingdom.

http://www.learn4good.com/arts-school.htm
A guide to art and design courses in the United Kingdom, United States, Canada, and Australia.

http://www.allartschools.com
A guide to art and design courses in the United States and Canada.

http://www.library.unisa.edu.au/resources
A list of art schools and colleges in Australia.

Index

Titles in the *Art off the wall* series include:

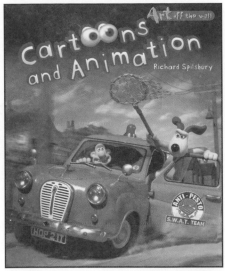

Hardback   978-0-431-01473-9

Hardback   978-0-431-01472-2

Hardback   978-0-431-01474-6

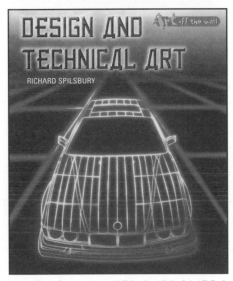

Hardback   978-0-431-01475-3

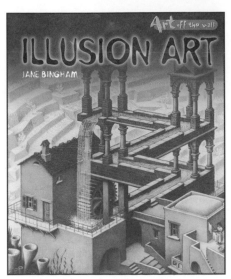

Hardback   978-0-431-01476-0

Find out about other titles from Heinemann Library on our website www.heinemann.co.uk/library